Field Guide

to

CAT BUTTS

T0364035

Running Press
Hachette Book Group
1290 Avenue of the Americas, New York, NY 10104
www.runningpress.com
@Running_Press

First Edition: May 2005

Published by Running Press, an imprint of Perseus Books, LLC,
a subsidiary of Hachette Book Group, Inc.

The publisher is not responsible for websites (or their content)
that are not owned by the publisher.

ISBN: 978-0-7624-2217-3

CONTENTS

Introduction

Domesticated house cats live all around us. There's probably one living in your house or at least one or more in your neighborhood that come around. These "cats" are nothing to be afraid of. In fact, they are wonderful creatures that happily share the world with us. There are many types or "breeds" of cats out there and sometimes it can be hard to distinguish one from another. One of the surest ways to identify a cat is through examination of its hind-quarter region otherwise known as its "butt."

This booklet provides a small sampling of cat butt images and helpful hunting hints to help you get started with the wonderful hobby of "cat watching and identification through the butt." The kit also includes a set of Cat Butt magnets that you can hang with pride on your refrigerator to show you are a true Cat Watcher!

How to

You'll find it surprisingly easy to get a good "view" of a cat's butt. Many times they show it on their own — and very close up!

hello!

Sitting at a computer or reading a book are two good ways to bait a cat. If there is a cat around and you are patient, he will inevitably walk up onto your lap or keyboard then suddenly raise up his tail and direct his hind quarters right towards your face. This is the perfect time to examine and identify the cat. It's very helpful to have a small notepad and pencil always ready.

★ Tip: *If you are out "in the field" and cannot be at a computer or with a book you can still get a cat to expose his butt by stroking his back firmly from neck to tail. As you stroke, his tail end should naturally pop right up.*

Congratulations on your new hobby! Have fun with it. You might even meet other enthusiasts and make new friends.

8

CAT BUTT SAMPLES

The following pages contain sample images of
particular cat butts and their descriptions.
Use these distinctive butts as a starting point.

American Shorthair

Although coat color and patterns may vary quite a bit, tabby is a common pattern. Males are significantly larger than females, weighing 11 to 15 pounds when fully grown. Mature females weigh 8 to 12 pounds when they achieve full growth at 3 to 4 years of age. American Shorthairs can live as long 15 to 20 years.

A common Shorthair anus is non-distinct and surrounded by a 1 to 2 inch halo of lighter colored fur.

Notes:

_____

_____

_____

_____

_____

_____

_____

American Shorthair

Siberian

Siberians have been around for more than a thousand years and their coat may be just about any color. They are considered a semi-long-hair with thick, rich fur in the winter and slightly less in the summer.

Siberians are not only rare, but they are also able to leap great distances. So getting a good "read" on their butt may be difficult.

A common Siberian anus, when found, tends to be flying through the air.

Notes:

_____

_____

_____

_____

_____

_____

_____

Siberian

Himalayan

This cat has a stocky body type, long hair, and placid temperament. The fur is so thick and soft, you might want to use their tail as a feather duster. Or maybe the whole cat like a car-wash mitt.

Their elegant anus is surrounded by thick, velvety fur that leaves nary a whisper of its presence visible from the outside world. To make a positive identification, you will need to push the fur aside to have a look-see.

Notes:

_____

_____

_____

_____

_____

_____

_____

Himalayan

Siamese

Siamese cats are vocal, lively and demanding. They are distinguished by their brilliant blue eyes and colored "points" (ears, face, tail and feet) which provide a striking contrast to the lightly colored body.

Equally striking is the anus, situated below the base of the tail. Often times, the anus is a brilliant color all its own.

It is not recommended to touch a Siamese on the anus directly.

Notes:

_____

_____

_____

_____

_____

_____

_____

16

Siamese

Black Cat

The black cat is distinguished by its color: Black. The tail is almost always a very dark color; black. The fur around the sides and along the spine also tend to be black. Oddly, though, the paws are often white, leading to the (sadly) high number of domesticated Black Cats to be named "boots". The Black Cat anus is a deep dark black—surrounded by a delicate circle of white fading into black.

Notes:

_____

_____

_____

_____

_____

_____

_____

Black Cat

Field Notes

Draw Here

Field Notes

Draw Here

Cat Butt Drawing Workshop

Use these two pages to refine your skills drawing cat butt
Start by sitting outside making purely gestural sketche
of cat's butts as they pass by. Test your skills by stoppir
strangers on the street and ask if they can tell the cat breed
by your anus sketches alone.

Draw more here:

GLOSSARY

Anal *Keeping meticulous notes and records regarding cat butts.*

Anus *Smallish opening just south of the cat's tail.*

Ass *We don't use this word.*

Aura *A secondary, larger halo.*

Busy Signal *When a cat can't be identified because he is using the cat box.*

Butt Munch *Getting bit by a cat as you examine the anus.*

Cat *Smallish, furry, four-legged animal similar to a dog but not.*

Cutting the Grass *Shaving a cat's halo for more accurate identification.*

Cyclops *Cat that exposes often.*

Dark Star *Cat that never exposes.*

Eclipse *When a cat unexpectedly performs STL on your computer keyboard or book, blocking your view of the book or monitor.*

Exposure *The state of a cat exposing the anus, particularly with extreme tail lift.*

Eye-of-the-Needle *Trying to identify a cat by examining the anus from afar.*

Eye-to-Eye *When a cat exposes extremely close to your face.*

Four-Eyes *Four cats exposing simultaneously.*

Full Moon *A large, bright white aura.*

Gimme *Cat that likes to be identified often and makes "eye-to-eye" contact.*

Halo *The inch or so of hair directly surrounding the anus area. Particular when its coloration varies from the rest of the cat.*

Hammer Down *When the tail is down during a tail lift, covering the anus.*

Heat *A cat's noisy, horny period. Good time to stay away.*

26

Heat Stroke *Stroking a cat while it is in heat. Not a good idea.*

Hind-Quarters *South end of a cat facing north.*

Hole in One *Quickly identifying a cat on the first try.*

Holes *Recent Disney movie starring Shia LaBeouf.*

Purr *The engine-like noise cats make when they are being stroked.*

Ski Lift *A person's hand stroking a cat as the cat goes into tail lift and the back goes into ski slope.*

Ski Slope *A cat's back during exposure and tail lift.*

Spelunker *Someone with an inordinate amount of interest in cat butts.*

Spontaneous Tail Lift (STL) *When a cat lowers his chest to the ground and curves his back in an inverted arc raising*

the tail and butt high into the air, exposing the anus. Particularly while NOT being stroked.

Stalking *Hanging out for too long in a certain area waiting for a particular cat to identify.*

Stroke *To rub a cat's back. From neck to tail is the proper direction.*

Tail *The part of the cat just above the anus that kind of looks like a leg sticking out the back without a paw.*

Tail Lift *When a cat lowers his chest to the ground and curves his back in an inverted arc raising the tail and butt high into the air, exposing the anus. Particularly as a result of being stroked.*

Touch and Go *Touching a Siamese cat on the anus and running away. Popular with pranksters.*

INDEX

CAT BUTT-ALOG

Full Size Magnet Set

Excellent reproduction of Cat Butt Illustrations by famed Cat Butt artist "Junichi." Magnetized for easy display on your fridge. Great gift idea for fellow Cat Butt enthusiasts.

Gum

Working hard in the field can take a toll on anyone's breath. Cat Butt Gum will help keep you fresh even on the longest days.

Air Freshener

When you are ready to get serious about your hobby, this is a great addition to your arsenal. Not scientifically proven, but people swear it makes cats expose when they smell it.